A KIND OF YELLOW

PATRICIA
LEE
LEWIS

D1059622

PATCHWORK FARM PRESS

WESTHAMPTON, MASSACHUSETTS

Grateful acknowledgement is made to the editors of the following publications, in which some of these poems first appeared: *The Berkshire Review*: "Two Hundred Wings," A Kind of Yellow," "Certain Words." *Crossing Paths, An Anthology of Poems by Women*, Mad River Press: "Exile." *The Women's Times*: "The Gift." Special thanks to *The Berkshire Review* for nominating "Two Hundred Wings" for a Pushcart Prize in Poetry; and to Dana Zeller-Alexis for producing "Honeysuckle," my performance of many of these poems to benefit the Miniature Theater of Chester.

COVER ART: *American Lotus*, pencil drawing by Bob Marstall. The American Lotus (*Nelumbo Lutea*) blooms in Texas and Massachusetts.

COVER AND BOOK DESIGN: Maureen Scanlon

Patchwork Farm Press
292 Chesterfield Road
Westhampton, Massachusetts 01027
www.writingretreats.org

ACKNOWLEDGEMENTS

Thanks to Pat Schneider, my esteemed mentor, and to my sisters and brothers in the large world of Amherst Writers & Artists; to my readers over the years, especially the gifted Diana Gordon; Susan Kan, Wally Swist, Jacqueline Sheehan, Sue Case, Cherrie Latuner, Richard Puchalsky; The ZerbyZerby Group: Ed Rayher, Mary Clare Powell, Carolyn Cushing, Susan Middleton, Gian Lombardo, Holly Iglesias; Deborah Dill, Beth Goren, Debora Seidman and Martha Olver; members of the Patchwork Farm Manuscript Group 2004: Alison Baker, Marianne Banks, Carolyn Benson, Portia Cornell, Sophy Craze, Mary Fussell, Sara Jonsberg, Ann McNeal; and all the Patchwork writers who have heard these poems raw; to my Vermont College colleagues and teachers, especially Jody Gladding, Cynthia Huntington, Richard Jackson, Mary Ruefle and Leslie Ullman.

Thanks to loving supporters and family: especially to John Henry Sackrey and Ponteir Sackrey, my beautiful, brave children; Ann Jones, Lyn Whitcomb, Susan Lewis, Don Wukasch, Bob Marstall, David Schellinger, Cie Simurro, Elliot Tarry, Jeffrey Leistyna, Cheri Cross, John Dearie, Jaimee Nalepinsky, Daniel Pikett, Christopher Sparks, Lisa Woody, Cari Clark, Priscilla Atherton, Mary Margaret Mueller, Nancy Banister; and to Carol Edelstein, who knows the whole story.

TO JOHN AND PONTEIR

IN MEMORY OF
WILLIAM JACK SACKREY, 1955–1976

CONTENTS

I. HONEYSUCKLE

HONEYSUCKLE

Momma made me go get a switch
from the honeysuckle bush
again today.

The first time it was because
I was playing doctor with Sarah
from across the street. We took off all

our clothes, even our panties,
so we could play with my new
doctor kit from my birthday.

It tickled when Sarah poked
me on my bottom with the shot.
We were giggling and rolling

on the grass when Momma came.
I picked the thinnest
branch I could find and pulled off

all the leaves. It stung my legs
like yellow jackets. Today, Momma
caught me playing doctor

with Davy from next door
and she hollered, "What
are you doing?" and I thought

she was going to cry
and she pulled my hand so hard
I left my doctor kit

in the yard all scattered.
This time, I pulled
a shorter branch that didn't whip

around so much and I left the leaves
on. Momma didn't like that.
She put her fist around it

and pulled it through her other hand.
Leaves fell all over the floor. Momma
switched and I danced, her hand

digging into my shoulder and me
trying to get out of that switch's
way. I cried and hollered,

Momma, don't, please Momma,
I promise I'll be good. Momma
says she wants me to be good

so when I grow up
I can be a doctor.

She sits her own horse and wild things
watch. She would do well to learn
from them. But she sees only herself. There
behind scrub cedar, the coyote
halts. He knows the light child, the proud eyes,
the pony. He sniffs the air. Trouble
is like disappointment: you'd better pay attention.
He turns, a slow curve into mesquite trees.
There's nothing to be gained.

The child yells for help. She is a frowning child,
accustomed to rebuke, and stubborn. She would rather
get down by herself, but it is far to the ground
and cactus needles wait everywhere. A screech owl
screams, shrugs a wing and flies
to pecan trees near the river. Jack rabbits flop,
ears in sunshine, translucent, but the child will not listen.

Diamondbacks slide beneath a cattle guard
by the caliche pit. If they would speak to her, they'd warn,
look out for varmints, child. Be still and watch
the changes. Prepare to lose
your skin. It is in this way that beauty comes.

SEVEN

Her pigtails pull against
her scalp as she lets her body go
in the early morning air.
The bar is cool
under her hooked knees, her arms
hang like legs, her heart
thumps in her ears.
She watches the world
upside down, how people bounce
when they walk, their mouths
like fishes. Mrs. Miller
walks across the backyard
for morning coffee with her mom,
bouncing like a kickball. Her brother
grabs her hair. You bully,
she calls, but she doesn't mean it,
really. He's her little brother.
He has black eyes. Her dress is up
around her shoulders, the Texas sun
warms her knees, her thighs, the place
between her legs she mustn't touch.
She hangs in space, unexplored,
a planet slowly spinning.

BLUE GLACIER

It is a mountain lake, and I am in the fir trees,
leaning. I am thirteen. We walked up here, my little sister
and brother. I am the oldest and I am in charge. My brother
has wild brown eyes, I have to watch him every minute.
My sister is good but she makes strangers smile
and they give her candy. My brother makes them laugh.
I have my period now and I won't go in the lake.
It is fed by the blue glacier. You can see it
above the fir trees. We went inside its cave and it was like
under deep water, the light was blue, the most blue
of the sky, and I was happy.

Today, my brother went into the lake. He swam
under the water and I could see him. His eyes were open
and dark. And then I couldn't see him and he didn't
come up, and I thought, he must love the blue light
so much. And then I thought, he is lost and I screamed out
into the lake, George, George, come up, like at home
when I call and call him for supper, a little mad. A man
dove in and I could see where mud came up like a storm
in the clear blue, and I could see him swimming back
and I could see my brother's dark brown head, but not
his eyes. His face was white like the snow on the glacier
and then he was face down on the wide flat rock and the man
pushed water from his mouth and then I saw him breathe.
And now I think if it would be good enough to die
like that, and if the blue is really blue
or is it just the sky I see from here.

TEXAS TWO-STEP

Uncle Blake, red nose, bright hooded eyes,
that funny smell I now know was booze,
I was crazy about you. *You can drive
this thing, Sugar, of course you can,*

*with those long legs of yours. Just git up
on that seat and push the pedals. I need
some help down at the River Corral. Don't
be a sissy, come on.* It was like being

set free: you cussed and drank and played
gin rummy until your head fell over, so
there weren't rules for me
either. Oh, Uncle Blake, I think you were

my first real love. But it wasn't you
I loved so much as it was me. When I was with you,
river stones sang, mesquite leaves shone silver
in the hot, yellow sun, and bleating sheep

moved slowly, eyes like amber watching
as we rode on by. And you could dance!
Like a great bear, light and swaying, belly
hopping over your belt buckle, caked boots

remembering the day's work: you'd grab me
and away we'd jump to a Texas two-step. It's a long time
since you died. These days, I have to remind myself
to watch light dawn on folded mountains

and not shade myself. But today, the sudden
thought of you, cussing, teasing, fills my belly like a sun;
and in its heat I toss my head and stretch
my legs and dance, heart hopping, with the bear.

The field stood
in its light, shimmering
from root and leaf. This
is how it was, he slammed
the dash board and the car screamed
through cactus thorns. This moon
had known the women
of the thousand fires, breasts
and heavy bellies burned
by blame. This is how it was,
this no-blood moon, in her sixteenth
year, in a shining pasture, on a summer night.

TWO HUNDRED WINGS

You are pregnant, the doctor says, I am sorry, leaves
float golden orange, he turns away, his white coat, his big
shoulders, between twig and ground, are you sure, the girl says,

a hundred starlings, it's all she can think to say, light
among red oak branches, except then she cries, their voices
like the voices of the thousand leaves, what else to do

with shame and sin and no one will forgive you now, beyond
the trees, you little whore, she can hear the baby's father,
a woman stands, except then, she says, inside the sobs she says,

she raises both her arms in salutation, is there anything you
can do, it being 1954, it being Texas, two hundred wings,
and this being unforgivable, he turns and says, a single

bellows whooshing, No, I'm sorry, and when her mother
slams her hands against the steering wheel, pushing air,
and says, what have you done to me, in close formation,

and when her father says, like a cloud, I will have to resign
from the ministry, she breathes the risen wind, she knows there
was nothing anyone could do, and she enters the cottage among trees.

THE FIST

Sheetrock splatters, edges, *goddam you, girl*, he yells,
the floor is cool, see how it shines, today she waxed
the new kind, liquid, under bed and dresser,
under bed, crawl under bed, it has clean sheets,
the new kind, corners fitted, pastel peach
and peaches just today hill country peaches
white and juicy, bruising easily, no peeling,
washing only, gently peaches under water,
smooth fuzz from stem, her mother
slices to the pit, again, and white
half-moons fall heaped and sweating, *get out*
from under there, you bitch, and get my dinner.
Chicken, fried, with good cream gravy,
biscuits like her gran's, and sweet canned peas.
Where is my dinner? Cobbler, thick peach
cobbler, back yard ice cream made by hand,
her daddy laughing, turning while the ice and salt
drip onto grass, come take a turn, you're getting
strong enough. Her momma fixing dinner, her daddy
home. Good job, go help your mother.
Setting plates and forks for six, the blessing
holding hands. *Get out of there, you bitch,*
I'll pull you by your ugly hair. Fuck the baby, you
pregnant whore. The screen door slams. June bugs hang
on with legs like jagged bolts. Outside the air
is cool against her arms, she's done the dishes and
can play a while. She leans against
the live oak tree and dreams of getting big
and getting married, making ice cream
in the dark, her kids, and all the blessings.

STRETCH MARKS

Tight as a globe, below the equator,
the skin splits apart. You,

who grow inside me like a tumor, you
cast marks of fire like worms

across my belly. Meanwhile, tonight,
my best friend is Queen of Homecoming.

Your father was the star in last year's
game. Don't look at my belly, don't look

at my breasts, look instead at my mouth
that never drops its smile. Worms throw

shadows on the belly of the world, our
Mother, play their games by starlight, casting

up the dead. The doctor's glasses slip
along his nose. The game is over,

and who cares, the sweating and the heavy
traffic. Please, dear belly, if I love you

without a whisper, isn't there somewhere
you can safely go?

The baby is coming.
It has not yet come.
It is coming.
The baby is huge in there.
Huge and mean. It is hurting her.
It does not want to be born.
It wants to go back.
It wants to kill her and go back.
God did not want her to have a baby.
She did an evil thing.
The baby wants her to give up.
It wants her to go away
and leave it alone.
It is not an angel anymore.
She has ruined it.
The baby knows her.
It knows her perfectly.

It will not let her be a child.
She is still a child.
There is still time to grow up.
The baby knows everything
and will punish her
forever and it will live an unnatural life,
for she has sinned.
The baby knows God
by heart.
God told the baby to enter her womb
and punish her.
The baby is torturing her now,
she cannot stop
screaming, no, no, no.
She wants the baby
to leave her alone.

It is better.

The baby is better now.

It knows her mind and her evil heart
and right now it is being nice to her.

But, now it is not.
It is cutting her stomach open.
It has a hunting knife and it is slicing her to bits.
The baby is strong, the baby
will not ever stop until she is dead.
It knows her evil thoughts.
It knows she is not forgiven.
It hears her voice in supplication to The Lord.
It laughs. Inside her belly
there is laughter,
hyena cries.
And she's its mother.
No, not yet, she is not a mother yet.

She is still a daughter.
There is still time
before her life is over,
but not much time,
the baby stirs again,
it doubles up its claws,
and polishes its scales.
Its eyes are orange.
They glint a spider's many lights.
It is too late.
She is betrayed.

Her belly opens, mouth
of rattlesnake,

venom squirts red,
and God's helpers
hover overhead.
They show their teeth,
they laugh.
A baby cries.
It is a baby now.
The air has sucked it
from her belly,
and it cries
like any baby,
red and warm, and small.

Steps are rough, paint peels gray to splinter, it will rain.
Toes are baby corn, sweet feet, not walking, knees
crawl pink on gray. Breathe, baby, bye-oh, baby
bunting, daddy's gone a'hunting, no rabbit skin, no

daddy, rain, oh bring the rain. Yellow hair is feathers,
baby chick with rivulets for cheeks; rain floods the creek;
baby falls like rain. Let me keep him safe. No growing up.
No breaking, only candy toes, ears soft as buttercups, lips

puckered against momma's neck. No world away
from porch, no hurting, never dying. No swinging,
branch already breaking, baby.

What does she do with the dark, this ideal woman?
Between preparing dinner in time
for her husband's return, in the middle of fixing
her makeup and ironing her hair ribbon, after
unfastening little, dirty hands from her hem, stuffing
children's mouths, where is her story? What
if he'd knocked out her tooth
last night? What if her smile doesn't
sparkle? What if the groceries cost more
than her allowance? Where will she go with the children
this time? The boss doesn't like him,
she understands why, but what can she say? Her mother
wore lipstick, so she wears it, too. It makes her
feel pretty. It smears when it hits the back
of his hand. She learns how to put it on, blot it, powder it,
put on some more. She always looks lovely. The dinner
is burning, children run through the kitchen, she's yelling, stop
slamming the door, your father will be here, you'd better be
quiet and clean and happy to see him. Great heavens,
the wash is still on the line. Between billowed sheets is
a world like a cloud. She hangs fully conscious from two great
    white sails—
oh, take me where somebody else does the smiling.
She reaches for clothespins and takes down the wash. There's room
in the linen closet for mothers. It's dark and quiet in there.

II. A KIND OF YELLOW

They let him out in my care for a few hours. It was the Thursday before Christmas and the stores were open until 9. I came straight from work to find that he had made an ornament, a train engine, red and blue glitter on styrofoam. *It looks like I made it when I was 7 instead of 20*, he said. *I am here for my son*, I said to the nurse. I remember putting my arm in his as we walked to my car. *I want to buy you a present, Mom. Where can we go?* He had money from his dad, he said, enough for me but not for anyone else. I pulled up in front of the department store. *Don't come in*, he said. He went inside. In 15 minutes he came out carrying a bag. He got in the car, looking straight ahead, frowning. *It's not the right one, Mom, I have to go back in. I have to.* I said, *I'm sure I'll love it. No*, he said, looking at me with hard, blue eyes. *It isn't the right color. OK*, I said, *I'll wait right here.* He went in. He came out. He got in the car and closed the door. He opened the door and got out. *It's the other one*, he said. *You'll like the other one better*, and slammed the door. He repeated this 5 times, each time his voice was louder, his eyes more brilliant. His fingers clutched the bag like a rope. The department store closed. He wept and I wept. *It's Christmas, Ma, and I can't stand that place. I want to be home with you and everybody. I want to give you the present now.* He opened the crumpled bag slowly, as though he didn't know what was there. He closed it quickly and said, *You won't like the color. I should have gotten the other one.* I said, *I will love the color. You picked it out. I will love the color.* The next day he cut his wrists. That time, he lived, but he never did come home.

EXILE

School-green linoleum, cracked;
gunmetal-gray steel bed; flat
steel springs; a mattress:
thin, plastic, warped. No sheets,
no blankets, nothing he can use

to harm himself. He paces
like a leopard on the cool, hard
floor. He throws his body
on the bed—I cannot catch him,

hold him. His mouth slams
the headboard and he slumps
to the floor. Blood is on the tongue
he rolls in and out, chest pushes

against knees, arms hold on.
I like it here, Mom,
he says, blue eyes smashed deep
in his head look straight at me.

I like it here, and that's
the terrible thing. But you see,
they didn't remember
to take away his belt, or

cover the steam pipes
running across the ceiling.
And he didn't really

mean he liked it *here*.

LIKE WILLOWS

This is the way I go to the window
when it is raining. These tears, the bending

forward to the knees, spatters on the sill. I walk
in small circles breathing rain from shingles

that no longer leak. You owed me nothing. Storms
have left the rivers filled and fertile. Your angry eyes are washed

to glistening. Wind becomes an ally of the forest. The demon
with one red eye told you to kill yourself, or someone else.

Pruning what is past its usefulness. I welcome wind
in all its strength. We walked together

from the game room at the hospital, the machines
of cigarettes and coffee and candy bars.

And sad souls who sit and rock their knees.
Hold out your arms for testing. Don't go, Mom, you said,

your face became the pleading darkness of the elevator door.
I don't remember walking out. The curse and bend.

Just feeling your strong arms one last time.
Like willows crossed.

A KIND OF YELLOW

It is always yellow, your color,
your hair, the light I saw when you were

born, yellow like raw silk, goldenrod
like laughter. Now, yellow moves on walls,

late afternoon, the time of day you died.
It's lovely here at home in winter. Sky so clear

the swollen moon should fall from lack
of holding. It's lovely, skeletons of oak

and birch and beech run black like ink
pulled wet across the tender yellow

sky. It's lovely here. You died
in February on a day so cold I huddled

in the bus toward home. Snow was yellow-
brown on roads, no sun. Not then, not

for a long, long time. In the hospital,
your hair was streaked as though by rivulets

of tears. The kitchen phone was ringing,
the voice dulled and yellow. It could not say

your son has hung himself, it said something
is wrong, Mrs. There is a kind of yellow

in a black-eyed Susan's heart, the tiny points of pollen
waiting. From these more flowers bloom

or honey flows, or mothers draw their sustenance
when spring arrives and something yellow grows.

UNICORN

Dirty clothes against the only
window, a poster on the stale gray wall,
the unicorn, fenced in a magic place,
with jeweled collar, all alone and
looking out. Your cotton underwear
in the pile and on them a dark,
brown crease. Maybe I should wash
them for your brother; but, no,
they are yours: it's your smell I smell;
the inside of your body; the diapers
I changed and washed by hand when both
of us were children. I find my face is pushed
into the cloth, my hands are claws, my face
the awful mother's face. My tears
make everything all wet, your underwear—
how weird—and yet they're all of you
I have: of the body I pushed out of mine,
the perfect ears and toes, the yellow hair.
These soiled and worn-out underpants
against my cheek are warm and wet
as if someone alive and whole and full
of breath were wearing them.

TRAFFIC LIGHT

If only the traffic light had been green,
if only the bus had been on time,
if I had taken an earlier bus,
if the seat beside me had not been vacant,
if I had not been so tired,
if lists of all I had to do had kept me alert,
if when I got home I hadn't taken off my shoes,
if I had driven straight to the hospital,
if I hadn't decided to wait for your brother,
if when the phone rang I had been on my way,
if I had not had good news I hoped would save you,
if when the phone rang, I had been opening your door,
perhaps you would not have hung so long from your belt,
perhaps I would have seen your face, perhaps
I could have held you in my arms.

whose wings beat back the wind when ashes
in a yellow box are all that remain? Curve

around me, wings of softly weeping. Listen.
Bare no sharp points. What fills the hole

when the grave is covered over? The vacancy
sign is propped in round river stones, but

it does not help. A young one fell from the nest
above the river and so the white bird

flies. She goes where red rocks take
the sun and make black holes across the desert.

Bones grow smooth in the burning
dark. Bones burned into ash are heavy as a child.

CERTAIN WORDS

Pouring, pouring, pouring, if I hold my hands this certain,
not quite touching, open to the sea breeze wind-breeze
waves soft as eyes of seals, gently water-wood,

through rain that angles hands not touching, fingers letting
water's sheen, pouring thickly, sweetly, rain like vinegar, like fire.
If I hold hands this certain, not quite touching, not quite holding,

not quite hands, this not quite certain way, if I remember eyes,
mouth sucking not quite touching, mouth wide open, body
hanging, not quite dying. If I hold my eyes this certain, not

quite looking, lids not closing, face not turning, if only
not quite touch him pouring, pouring, eyes of sapphires,
eyes of caves, the hands wide open, mouth like momma,

momma. If I not quite grasping, stroking, if I certain
breathing, beating heart. If I not quite hold my heart,
the pouring, pouring, pouring, he is with me, never leaving,

nothing staying, nothing weeping, nothing pouring,
pouring, letting, letting. If I hold my mouth the certain words,
graceful, words the grateful, if not quite holding, pouring,

pouring, let the thankful, thankful, thankful.

You know saddle leather creaking dry, boots bent elfin
at the toes, and dust. And you know mourning doves.

Their soft, cool cries are the lament you cannot speak.
Turkeys call from roosts along the river in the tops of wild pecans.

The river dies in pools of limestone rock and turtles edge
a little further under banks. It's by the great pecans

you'll bury the ashes of your son. The light
grows out of ground like grass. There is so little grass. Earth

light begins in silver pods of thorny, sweet mesquite and shivers
out of crimson cactus pears. It follows lines of tawny cedar

fence posts, travels rust and rich along barbed wire to spangle
horses' eyes. By mid-day nothing moves away

from shadows of pecans along the river or from patterned
shelter of squat live oaks. All is waiting. Will the evening

come again? Can light so white and upright lean to purple
and the reds that slant across the world? At noonday, when

light is all there is, there is no breathing. Nothing sings
or cries or barks. What fills the body is the light

grown like a god, and who can speak to that? There is sighing
when the light gives way, returns to earth, its shadow

like a cloak laid gently down, and something dies. In morning,
when light sprouts silver, you will bury him, and you will visit there

in evening light, and hear the clear bronze voice of turkeys,
and the doves begin to murmur in the cedar breaks.

SOMETIMES WAKING UP

And in a dream, my first-born child, dead
over twenty years, walks ahead of me—

I am keeping close, not to lose him again—
wide shoulders, straight, muscled back,

ridge visible across the scapula where he
usually has wings. I think: Of course,

they are detachable. Sometimes
waking up is trusting

the turning of the night
isn't in your hands.

Do not regret the diapers, lean to the window
above the sink, catch a glimpse
of zinnia, flaming yellow. Do not regret
the sink, the diapers, the window's dusty screen, you were not
nearly old enough. Do not regret the mornings
without the leaning tree, think of willow brush along the draw.

Rise up among the trees, acorns when your child
was born, saplings when he died. Find stones to mark
your stories in the mountain laurel groves;
invite all wanderers to rest.

Remember washing diapers in an old chipped sink.
They whipped the line and smelled of cloud. Remember
bark between your toes, the branch you lay on,
balancing. Remember the child
who had a child and kissed his feet.

Air taut and crisp as a new apple, wool hat itchy over ears, she follows the path behind the house. So much to do. Open door to cellar, lay last year's 2x4s along the back wall, rake lines into dirt floor, breathe dust, mold, sneeze. A mask? No, let me loose, she says. When lifting, bend the knees, listen to the creak and snap of tendon, feel hamstrings tighten; when bending, engage abdominals, remember where they are. She pulls on leather gloves, red stripe across the wrists, and pushes toward the stack, wheelbarrow, gray, its shoulders like a mule's, already tired. Position wheel and legs, the balance point. She trembles, stutters, nothing comes of it. No tears, there's work to do. She loosens hands, moves arms together, finds a modest piece, well-split, remembers breathing fumes, the splitter's roar, hands not hesitating, stick by stick, the pile. She takes one piece of wood, and puts it back. Another, birch, part of the old forked tree above the house: why burn that piece, it's perfect; and the next, the ash, straight, clean, like sculpture, carved to purity. Her breath is short, she sits, ground cold and hard enough to hold a house; she puts her head on knees; a nuthatch fusses from the ginkgo tree. I know, she says, I have to and I will, and still she sits, her head in gloves with red around the wrist. It's that, she says, the red, I will not think of him, the razor blade, the first time, the voice, a baby bird, *Mom*, a morning cold and clear. She hits the ground with palms protected by their leather gloves. You sissy, she says to herself, and she staggers, grabs the birch, throws hard. Wheelbarrow wobbles, stands; ash, oak, the barrow filling, her heart gains ground. The nuthatch rasps its single winter note.

I would be a woman mad with courage,
a moon on palm leaves, a lotus spreading,
a lily of the field, rejoice and weep. I would open.
I would bless my children with my stillness, a mountain lake;
invite them to bathe, each one magnificent.
Find stories in the ashes planted among trees.
I would hold their power in one hand,
the other yielding, sky to stars.
I would listen to the stories where they wait
in tawny creeks and live oak trees that lean,
on altars where preachers look like fathers,
in sewing rooms where mothers rip
their skirts to make new clothes, in rooms where children
birth their babies, in campfires, old church
songs, in bodies growing strong as cats
and minds as quick as wings inside a trumpet vine,
in turtle rivers green with Texas sun, in padlocked rooms
where those whose souls are claimed
by demons live and die. I would be mad
with wonder, alive with love of darkness and of light.
I would be this one here, this plain decaying
body in this loud, expanding heart.